Scott Hamilton

Additional Titles in the Sports Reports Series

Andre Agassi
Star Tennis Player
(0-89490-798-0)

Troy Aikman
Star Quarterback
(0-89490-927-4)

Roberto Alomar
Star Second Baseman
(0-7660-1079-1)

Charles Barkley
Star Forward
(0-89490-655-0)

Jeff Gordon
Star Race Car Driver
(0-7660-1083-X)

Wayne Gretzky
Star Center
(0-89490-930-4)

Ken Griffey, Jr.
Star Outfielder
(0-89490-802-2)

Scott Hamilton
Star Figure Skater
(0-7660-1236-0)

Anfernee Hardaway
Star Guard
(0-7660-1234-4)

Grant Hill
Star Forward
(0-7660-1078-3)

Michael Jordan
Star Guard
(0-89490-482-5)

Shawn Kemp
Star Forward
(0-89490-929-0)

Mario Lemieux
Star Center
(0-89490-932-0)

Karl Malone
Star Forward
(0-89490-931-2)

Dan Marino
Star Quarterback
(0-89490-933-9)

Mark McGwire
Star Home Run Hitter
(0-7660-1329-4)

Mark Messier
Star Center
(0-89490-801-4)

Reggie Miller
Star Guard
(0-7660-1082-1)

Chris Mullin
Star Forward
(0-89490-486-8)

Hakeem Olajuwon
Star Center
(0-89490-803-0)

Shaquille O'Neal
Star Center
(0-89490-656-9)

Scottie Pippen
Star Forward
(0-7660-1080-5)

Cal Ripken, Jr.
Star Shortstop
(0-89490-485-X)

David Robinson
Star Center
(0-89490-483-3)

Barry Sanders
Star Running Back
(0-89490-484-1)

Deion Sanders
Star Athlete
(0-89490-652-6)

Junior Seau
Star Linebacker
(0-89490-800-6)

Emmitt Smith
Star Running Back
(0-89490-653-4)

Frank Thomas
Star First Baseman
(0-89490-659-3)

Thurman Thomas
Star Running Back
(0-89490-445-0)

Chris Webber
Star Forward
(0-89490-799-9)

Tiger Woods
Star Golfer
(0-7660-1081-3)

Steve Young
Star Quarterback
(0-89490-654-2)

Jim Kelly
Star Quarterback
(0-89490-446-9)

Jerry Rice
Star Wide Receiver
(0-89490-928-2)

SPORTS REPORTS

Scott Hamilton

Star Figure Skater

Barry Wilner

Enslow Publishers, Inc.

40 Industrial Road   PO Box 38
Box 398   Aldershot
Berkeley Heights, NJ 07922   Hants GU12 6BP
USA   UK

http://www.enslow.com

Library of Congress Cataloging-in-Publication Data

Wilner, Barry.
    Scott Hamilton: star figure skater / Barry Wilner.
        p. cm. — (Sports reports)
    Includes bibliographical references (p.   ) and index.
    Summary: A biography of the accomplished figure skater, Scott Hamilton,
who was inducted into the World Figure Skating Hall of Fame in 1990.
    ISBN 0-7660-1236-0
    1. Hamilton, Scott, 1958– —Juvenile literature. 2. Skaters—United
States—Biography—Juvenile literature. [1. Hamilton, Scott, 1958– . 2. Ice
Skaters.] I. Title. II. Series.
GV850.H33W55   1999
796.91'2'092—dc21
[b]   98-35035
                                                                   CIP
                                                                    AC

Printed in the United States of America

10 9 8 7 6 5 4 3 2 1

To Our Readers:
All Internet addresses in this book were active and appropriate when we
went to press. Any comments or suggestions can be sent by e-mail to
Comments@enslow.com or to the address on the back cover.

Photo Credits: AP/Wide World Photos, pp. 17, 19, 28, 44, 51, 54, 63, 66, 68,
75, 77, 81, 87, 90

Cover Photo: AP/Wide World Photos

Contents

Chapter 1

Hamilton's Greatest Triumph

I win!" Scott Hamilton stood at center ice of the Great Western Forum in Los Angeles, a huge smile lighting up his face—and the whole arena. Around him, some ten thousand people were on their feet, cheering, clapping, sending out waves of love toward the skater.

It was October 29, 1997, and Hamilton had just finished his first performance since fighting a six-month battle with testicular cancer. Simply being on the ice was a victory for the 1984 Olympic gold medalist who had charmed fans all over the world ever since.

It did not even matter that he fell during the show. The fact that he was healthy, recovered from the cancer, and on the ice—where he belonged—was the only important thing.

Said Hamilton,

> I went for it and, well, you saw what happened but it was OK, too, because you can't land something unless you try it. It was so emotional for me. It was hard to focus, concentrate and get back into performance mode. I haven't been there in a while.[1]

For more than six months, Scott Hamilton had been off the ice, spending time in hospitals and clinics and at home. He was treated with many different medicines. He even had surgery to remove a tumor that was once the size of two grapefruits, and spent long periods just resting. Fighting cancer was the hardest thing he had ever done.

Scott had seen his mother, Dorothy, die of cancer when he was eighteen years old. He had seen her suffer from the disease, yet she was always strong for him. He knew he could not let cancer beat him. He would be strong through the treatments that would lead to his recovery.

He said:

> My mother died of cancer, and I saw what she went through and saw how brave she was, and that was a major factor [for me] in facing it without crumbling. That was a great source of

inspiration. Another is I just don't like losing. I understand if someone is better than me on a given day, OK. But this is one thing doctors said is treatable, and pretty much the more I participate and the more confidence I have and the more optimistic I am, the more likely I would come through this without any other effects.

The doctors are a lot smarter than I am. They didn't negotiate their high school diplomas. I did. [Scott completed high school studies through courses at home and tutoring.][2]

Hamilton was on tour in early March 1997 with Discover Card's Stars on Ice (a show he had created twelve years earlier) when he began to feel ill. On March 15, in East Lansing, Michigan, his stomach and his back were hurting and he had trouble jumping. A physical therapist told him, "You need to have this checked out" after feeling something hard and tight and as big as a ball in his groin.[3]

But first, Scott skated one more show, even though by the end, the pain was so bad, he could barely stand up straight. The next day, in Peoria, Illinois, he went to a hospital for tests. A doctor told him he had a tumor and that it should be taken care of right away.

Said Hamilton:

When somebody tells you you have something like this, it is an instant shock, and you get a huge lump in your throat. It's hard to say at first, "This is happening to me." But I had a pretty quick turnaround. Then, it was, "All right, this happened, what next? How do I fight it and beat it? Give me all the information and what it takes to get rid of this thing."[4]

Getting rid of this thing would take a lot of doing. First, Hamilton told the other skaters in the show, some of his closest friends, what was wrong.

"This is someone everybody loves," said Ekaterina Gordeeva, whose husband, Sergei Grinkov, had died of a heart attack only one and a half years earlier. "We all cried when we heard it, but we knew Scott would fight back and recover." Added Rosalynn Sumners, the only skater left on the tour who had been there when Scott began Stars on Ice, "We had not heard any complaints from Scott. We were at a rehearsal and Scott wasn't there and he never missed rehearsals. So we said, 'Where is he?'" Someone said he was at the hospital for some tests. "When he came back to the arena, he was limping and pale and he looked terrible." Sumners added, "I called my fiancé, who said he already knew and that we should do the show before Scott told us anything. I knew then it was serious. I watched Scott's face all night."[5]

But Hamilton did not let the audience know that he was very ill. Instead, he had a super performance.

Hamilton told *People* magazine:

> When I got on the ice that night, the reality of the situation was setting in. I was frightened, because I didn't know what was growing inside me. And I was depressed, because I knew this could be my last show of the year. Then I thought that if this thing was serious, this could be my last show ever.[6]

No way. Scott Hamilton would fight to make sure it was only a short break in his career. It would, however, be a painful, lonely time. Hamilton's business manager, Bob Kain, arranged for him to go to the Cleveland Clinic Foundation, one of the top cancer centers in the United States, to begin treatments. Hamilton's girlfriend, Karen Plage, flew from her home in Denver to be by his side.

The clinic put Scott Hamilton on a program in which he would have four cycles of chemotherapy, a series of treatments that use chemicals to shrink the tumor. Then he would have surgery to remove what was left of the disease.

Hamilton would not be back to tour with the other skaters for the rest of the season. The tour was in Dayton, Ohio, when the skaters found out Scott

Hamilton would not return for any more shows that year.

Said Kristi Yamaguchi:

> We had to let Scott know how much he means to us and how much we supported him. Scott always has inspired me because, even if I felt too tired to practice or rehearse, he was always there, working hard to make everything go right. So how could I not do the same thing? We went there to tell him that he was always there for us and we were going to always be there for him.[7]

FACT

During his comeback performance at the Los Angeles Forum, Scott Hamilton fell while performing a triple toe loop. The crowd, including actor Jack Nicholson and model Cindy Crawford, reacted to Hamilton's mistake with applause.

Hamilton's first treatment involved taking six hours of shots of chemicals for five days. The chemicals would burn up everything they touched, but the healthy cells inside Hamilton's body would recover. His appetite was strong during these treatments, and he even gained weight because of all the liquids he was receiving. He said the first stage of chemotherapy "wasn't terrible" for him.

After returning to his Denver home, he began taking a drug that made him feel very sick. These were some of the worst times. Scott Hamilton, "Mr. Energy," wanted to do nothing but lie in bed, sleep, and be alone.

He said:

> Even when friends or my family wanted to visit, I wasn't up to it. I knew there were

hundreds and hundreds of messages and notes and letters from people, but I didn't even feel up to going through them. I felt great about people caring so much and reaching out to show me their love and support, but I also was struggling with the treatments.[8]

It was just before the second round of chemotherapy that Scott Hamilton and his girlfriend made a big decision: Because his hair was falling out from the treatments, they decided to shave Hamilton's head. Sure, he was already balding, but what was left of his hair was part of his charm. He would have a different look when he returned to the ice, as he knew he would someday. "I just didn't want the cancer to win," he said.[9]

The second cycle of treatments was no worse than the first and Hamilton said, "I remember thinking it was a breeze. 'I'm good at cancer, I can do this.' But I would feel worse during the third and fourth cycles."[10]

Scott Hamilton headed for Los Angeles in April, hoping for some warmer weather. He even felt good enough to play some golf. On May 2, the third round of treatments began. "The doctors had warned me the third treatment would be the worst," he said. "And they were right. By the third day . . . I was a slug."[11]

During those treatments, Scott Hamilton kept remembering that he was more than halfway through. If he could use the same determination that made him an Olympic champion, he would get past this. He would get back on the ice.

Late June brought another major challenge: surgery to remove the tumor, which now had shrunk to the size of a golf ball. Scott admitted it was the toughest time of all. But, after the surgery, he would be able to say the cancer was out of his body. He could begin training for a return to skating. He said:

> I was scared out of my mind until we got into the operating room and they were playing rock music and hurrying around and it was like another day at the office. At first, when you find out it's cancer, it is very, very scary. But there are lots of alternatives now with medical advances.[12]

Doctors made a long cut from just below the chest to just above the groin, with a little loop around the belly button. Another cut was made in the groin area, and the tumor was removed.

Scott Hamilton was in the hospital in Cleveland for eight days. He was unable to eat solid food. He lay in bed most of the time, because it was too painful to sit up. He was tired much of the time. But he was also getting healthier.

"Since then, I'm just trying to get well and stronger," he said in early July after heading back home to Denver, where he would spend another month taking it easy. "Each day, I feel a little better, but it is a lot for a body to go through."[13]

By August 1, he was given the go-ahead to resume skating, although just in short sessions. There would be no jumping, no spinning, no splits. There would be only simple stroking, the kind of skating he had done when he got started as an eight-year-old.

Hamilton said of stepping back on the ice:

> It took time to muster my courage. I decided my mind would know how to do everything, but my body wouldn't. So I started breaking in new skates, which always limits how much you try. But it was double-whammy time: I was uncoordinated and very weak. It was not a very pleasant experience.
>
> Actually, it was devastating that first day back. I couldn't do anything. I got dizzy when I would spin. My balance was shot.[14]

FACT

The challenging move for Hamilton during his comeback show was the back flip. He performed it, despite an incision from his cancer surgery that runs several inches—from just below his chest to his abdomen.

Slowly, though, everything came back to Scott Hamilton. First, it was the footwork. Then a few spins. Then some easier jumps. Within a week, he was doing double jumps.

He still needed to build up his stamina. Getting tired quickly was something he expected, but it also was hard to deal with. And he was not close to being ready for a show. Yet he was already planning one.

For a decade, Scott Hamilton had worked with the Make-A-Wish Foundation. This group grants the wishes of seriously ill children. Through the Stars on Ice tour and many other appearances, Scott had raised millions of dollars for Make-A-Wish. So he knew how to raise money for worthy causes. Now he wanted to do the same for the Cleveland Clinic that had helped him. But how?

He would recruit many of his skating friends, former Olympians such as Ekaterina Gordeeva, Rosalynn Sumners, Kristi Yamaguchi, Kurt Browning, Brian Boitano, Katarina Witt, and Paul Wylie, to perform in a benefit for the clinic.

The main part of the show would feature those skaters performing some of Scott Hamilton's most famous skits. The skaters all loved the idea, and so did Hamilton.

Brian Boitano, the 1988 Olympic men's champion and the only male skater in the United States who could rival Hamilton in popularity, had this to say of Hamilton:

> His role in skating is so established from his great performances through the years. A lot of people win the Olympics and then they sort of rest on their laurels. He keeps trying to push to

Scott Hamilton worked hard to prepare for his first show after beating cancer. Here he is rehearsing for his "Festival on Ice" appearance in southern California, February 2, 1988.

do different things and in different directions and Scott has improved as a pro. He's developed so many routines that everyone remembers. So we all jumped at the chance to play Scott.[15]

The show was set for October 29, 1997. As Hamilton worked to get ready, he discovered that, yes indeed, he still had the drive to succeed, the boost that had made him a champion. He said:

I want to retire on my terms. I don't want this episode to stop me from skating. When I no longer enjoy it, I will stop. I was really enjoying it last year, having a great year. I love my job and that is inspiration enough.

Being a skater and seeing people and being able to entertain them means a great deal to me. It has given me pride and pleasure, and I'm not ready to give that up. I have the opportunity to entertain, and it's one I take very seriously.

I feel more at home on the ice than I do at home. For me, heaven is on the ice.[16]

Scott Hamilton watched as his friends performed his routines on ice at the Great Western Forum that wonderful night in late October. Then he put on his skates and, to a warm, loud ovation from the adoring crowd, he performed.

"I knew I wasn't 100 percent, but I just had to be

Scott Hamilton raises his arms in triumph after returning to the ice on October 29, 1997, in Inglewood, California. This was his first performance since being diagnosed with testicular cancer earlier in the year.

out there one more time," he said. "It was magic and I'll never forget it as long as I live."[17]

Nor would anyone who was there, including saxophonist Kenny G. and singer Olivia Newton-John, who performed as part of the show.

"I admire him very much for coming back so quick," said Newton-John, herself a breast cancer survivor. "He'll be fine. I have no doubts."[18]

No one else could doubt it, either, when Hamilton had finished his inspirational routine.

He skated to "With One More Look At You," sung in person by his friend, Gary Morris. "It wasn't my best. It wasn't about being 100 percent. It was about standing between these lights and having the greatest view in the world."[19]

Chapter 2

Childhood Years

Scott Hamilton never knew his biological parents. He was born in Toledo, Ohio, on August 28, 1958, and was put up for adoption.

Dorothy and Ernie Hamilton lived in Bowling Green, Ohio, where Ernie taught at the state university and Dorothy was a second-grade teacher. The Hamiltons had one daughter, Susan, who was five and a half years old. They decided to adopt a brother for Susan, and Scott came into their lives in October 1958.

Susan wondered why the baby was so wrinkled. She asked about taking home a different baby. She soon warmed to the idea that Scott was going to be her younger brother, however. It was not long before she brought the baby to school for show-and-tell.

From the beginning, the energy that has made Scott such a special performer was part of his personality. He walked early and soon was moving so quickly that his parents and sister sometimes had trouble keeping up with him.

Scott loved to climb. His father had to build a top to his crib to keep him from climbing out as soon as an adult left the room. Once, Scott's father was working on the roof of the house. The ladder was standing at the side of the house. Suddenly Scott, then two years old, was walking along the edge of the roof.

On another occasion, Scott's mother heard laughter coming from above the refrigerator, inside a pantry. She knew even before she opened the doors who was giggling inside. "I guess I was a pretty active little guy," Scott said with his infectious smile.[1]

When he was about four years old, Scott gained a brother when, in 1962, the Hamiltons adopted Stephen. By then, it had been explained to Scott that he, too, had been adopted.

The busy Hamilton household also included lots of pets. Scott brought home animals all the time. He also tried skating for the first time, on a frozen driveway. He remembered:

> We were holding on to a car and we were skating around a car. I fell off my skates and landed on my head and cried for two hours. I just wanted those things off my feet. I said I would never put them on again. I never wanted to skate again.[2]

Scott would not get on skates again for a long time. But he had another problem to deal with. He was not growing at a normal rate. His parents had actually been speaking to doctors about the problem ever since Scott was two years old. When Scott was nearly five, he entered kindergarten and did well. Teachers, other students, and parents all liked him. He made them laugh.

But there would not be much laughter in Scott's life beginning in first grade. Doctors put him on a special diet to help his growth, and he hated it. He had to give up milk and dairy products, and lots of sweets. When his friends ate cookies or candy, Scott had jelly rolls made with rice flour. The only thing he really liked was being able to drink cola all the time to keep up his energy level.

Along with not growing, Scott began losing weight. He spent weeks at the hospital being tested. He could not go out and play with his friends when he was at home because he was too weak. He could not keep up with the other kids.

As a second-grader, Scott was so small he had to sit at a first-grader's desk—when he could make it to school. During recess, while other students played ball and tag outside, Scott sat in the classroom, playing with toys.

But he rarely complained. He had to drink a pink liquid he described as "yucky," but he drank it in hopes it would make him feel better. Doctors even put a feeding tube into his stomach. It came out through his nose and was hooked up to a bottle of liquid.[3]

By the time he was in third grade, Scott's outlook was very dark. Some doctors told Scott's mother that Scott was going to die. Some said he had cystic fibrosis, a deadly disease. Others said that he had celiac disease, a rare disease that affects the ability to digest foods and made Scott's strange diet necessary. But they could not find a diet that would help him grow or keep his weight up.

Throughout Scott's life, people have been kind to him, mainly because of his friendliness, his politeness, and his cheerful attitude. One of the most important people to Scott was a family friend, Dr. Andrew Klepner. He lived nearby and was the family doctor.

Dr. Klepner was sure Scott had none of those diseases. He even believed Scott did not need a special diet. And he proved it. The families were on a weekend holiday when Dr. Klepner told Scott to eat whatever he wanted. Scott was afraid, at first. But he took a few bites of different foods (donuts, ice cream), and soon was eating normally.

He did not begin to grow any quicker, though. And more hospital tests could not come up with a reason. Again, doctors said it was cystic fibrosis. Again, Scott was stuck in hospital beds. It was getting hard for everyone to smile. And, again, Dr. Klepner helped.

During Christmas vacation of 1967, the Hamiltons went to Boston. Dr. Klepner arranged for Scott to go to the Children's Hospital. It is considered one of the best hospitals in the world. The doctor was sure that Scott could be cured of whatever illness he had. He was right. Scott spent four days at the hospital, where doctors found that Scott had a partially paralyzed intestine. (The intestine, located behind the stomach, digests food after the food has passed through the stomach.) With the proper diet—no more "yucky" stuff—and exercise, doctors felt the problem could be corrected. The exercise was figure skating, and Scott would come to love it.

FACT

Scott Hamilton has always had a fondness for pets, especially cats, that dates back to his childhood. Among the animals in the Hamilton household were a succession of cats named Puffy Buttons.

The university where Scott's father taught opened a new skating rink. Dr. Klepner signed up his children for a Saturday morning skating club. Susan Hamilton went along. Scott had seen a skating show when he was in Boston. He thought he would like to try getting on the ice, too.[4]

"I remember holding onto the boards for a long time and just stroking around," he said. "Maybe I was afraid or maybe it just felt weird. But I do know I soon started to get away from the boards and it was great fun."[5]

No one could have known that skating would actually save Scott's life. He began going to the rink regularly. At age nine, he started private lessons with Rita Lowery, his first coach. A few weeks later, at a doctor's checkup, Scott had grown more than an inch. He had also gained weight, and was eating normally. He no longer was getting sick. He did not need to miss school or spend full days in bed.

The exercise from skating put Scott on the road to good health. Scott was a bundle of energy on the ice. He could not learn jumps and spins quickly enough.

The Hamiltons were so thrilled about Scott's improved health that they encouraged him to become more involved. He took longer lessons as his mother and father scraped together the money to pay for them. Skating is a very expensive sport. For the next decade, Scott's parents would do everything they could to pay for it.

Said Hamilton, "My parents made some amazing sacrifices for me. Everything I've done in skating is because they believed in me and worked so hard to help me succeed."[6] And succeed he did. He ignored the teasing by others that figure skating was "a sissy sport." He did play hockey for a while. He was even knocked out once during a game. But his "game" was skating.

He did his best in school while putting so much time into skating. But, as he admitted years later, "I never was going to be a straight-A student."[7] Skating gave him the confidence he did not have when he was sickly and often on his own. Scott began passing figure skating tests, learning the compulsory figure eights (a skating pattern in which a performer skates in a pattern resembling an eight) that must be traced on the ice. He mastered tougher jumps and showed off a bit.

By 1969, Scott was winning competitions on the lowest levels, subjuvenile and juvenile. When he made his first long-distance skating trip to California, he came in second in individual competition and third in ice dancing. But ice dancing

Scott Hamilton performs a back flip at Wollman Rink in Central Park in New York City, February 2, 1994. The former Olympic gold medalist was joined by fellow Olympians Kristi Yamaguchi and Paul Wylie and ten children from the Make-A-Wish Foundation. The skaters were rehearsing for an upcoming "Discover Stars on Ice" appearance in New York.

would not last long. Scott was still small and there were few girls his size to be his partner.

Scott's mother eventually taught at Bowling Green University, along with his dad. The extra money she earned helped pay for the increasing expenses of skating. Scott's mom also went with him on his many trips. She tutored him and enjoyed his recovery and new life with him.

Scott attracted national attention after a local news story spread to other areas of the country. The headline for the story read "Ice Skating Uplifts Life of 'Miracle Child.'"

He had a new coach, Giulano Grassi, who helped him learn some of the basics of the sport. Grassi stayed with Scott for less than a year, however.

Scott's next coach, Herb Plata, helped him put some flair into his skating. Plata had been in "Holiday on Ice," a touring show. Scott told him he would like to do the same thing someday.[8] (Someday, he would, in fact, be the headliner on the most popular tour in figure skating.)

First, Scott needed to move up the ladder, through juvenile (which he reached at the end of 1969), to intermediate, novice, junior, and senior. He would need to win regional and sectional competitions in order to reach the national championships.

The first major step came at the 1970 Eastern

Great Lakes Regionals, where Scott won. From regionals, the top skaters go to sectionals. If they win medals there in novice, junior, or senior, they qualify for the United States Figure Skating Championships. (There is no intermediate level at the United States Championships.)

Scott had to take the third-level figure skating test four times. But he did well when he finally passed it and went from the juvenile level to the intermediate level. He won compulsories at the Eastern Great Lakes. It was an amazing win after all the trouble he had had passing the test. Excited from doing that, he also won the overall title in his first intermediate event.

That sent him to Midwestern Sectionals, where he was third. Scott had become popular in the sport. He was also making appearances throughout the country. He even traveled to Toronto, Canada, for a competition.

The national championships became a goal in 1972. It was at that time that Scott moved up to novice. Before family, friends, and supporters in Bowling Green, he won regionals. At thirteen, he was within reach of joining the very best figure skaters at the United States Championships in Long Beach, California. He barely missed. After finishing third in compulsories and also in the technical program, he took fourth overall in the sectional competition at Minneapolis. It was the first major disappointment of his skating career. But it also showed Scott and his parents that the talent was there. They always knew the desire was there. It was time to think on a grander scale. Scott was among the big boys now.

Chapter 3

The First Olympics

Big decision time had arrived for the Hamiltons. While Scott was skating at sectionals, his parents spoke to many people about their son. Was he good enough to be a champion some day? Did he need a famous coach? Had he outgrown Bowling Green?

The answers they got were all the same: yes. So the Hamiltons made one of the most difficult decisions of their lives. They agreed to send Scott to a place where he could get top-level coaching and build his skills. Just a few years before, the Hamiltons had wondered whether Scott would live. Now, they wondered whether he was headed toward fame and glory.

In the summer of 1972, Scott headed to Rockton, Illinois, where he would be coached by Pierre

Brunet at the Wagon Wheel rink. "It was a very big decision for all of us," Scott said.

> It would be the first time I was living away from home. My parents had to think about school, about the money it would cost, about not being with me all the time. For a thirteen-year-old and for his mother and father and sister and brother, it was a major decision.[1]

Scott's parents sold their house and moved to a smaller one. They used much of the money they made to pay for Scott's skating.

The Wagon Wheel rink was home to Janet Lynn, America's skating queen at the time. Also training there was Gordie McKellen. He would win the next three United States men's championships—and also become something of a big brother to Scott.

Was Scott uncomfortable in a place with such big stars? Did he hold Janet Lynn and Gordie McKellen in awe? Not at all. In fact, some days it was more like a summer camp than a training ground. Scott liked to pull practical jokes on friends. He became sort of a class clown off the ice.

But he was learning quickly under the teaching of Coach Pierre Brunet. Brunet had worked with many great skaters around the world during his fifty-year career. Scott got much better at doing figure eights. He would build on what he learned in

Rockton to become one of the best tracers of figure eights in men's skating.

Coach Brunet also understood that Scott needed programs that let him entertain while he competed. The coach wanted Scott's personality to show. So he put together routines that were fun for Scott and for the audience.

It was not only Coach Brunet who boosted Scott when he came to Rockton. Gordie McKellen had also been to many important competitions. While he was in training for nationals, he spent time with Scott. They talked about what it was like to compete at such a high level. They also talked about skating in front of huge crowds or on television.

"He took me under his wing and showed me things," Scott said of Gordie, who was five years older. "He developed the fight. I never was much of a fighter until Gordie."[2]

While Gordie McKellen was heading to his first United States championship, Scott Hamilton was also breaking through. He won regionals at Columbus, Ohio, with his parents and many friends and neighbors in the crowd cheering him on. He won sectionals in Denver, earning his first trip to nationals. He would become a familiar face and a key figure at the United States Figure Skating Championships for many years. In his first try, however, he wound up ninth in Minneapolis—dead last among novice men.

"At least Gordie won," Scott remembered. "That kind of inspired me and made me realize if I worked hard, I wouldn't be last all the time. I could be first, too."[3] Not for a while, though.

In 1974, Scott won sectionals again. It was his third year at the novice level. He knew he had to move up to juniors soon. He wanted to do so as a national champ, but he was still just dreaming of that. He went to Providence, Rhode Island, for nationals. While Gordie won again, Scott was ninth out of ten.

By now, a little doubt had crept into Scott Hamilton's mind. He began wondering whether he was good enough. Then, during the summer, he jumped out of his bunk bed and broke his right ankle. Improving his skating took a backseat to getting healthy. He could not skate with a cast on.

But the broken ankle was not the worst news Scott would get that year. His mom was diagnosed with breast cancer. She had surgery, and a long battle with the disease had begun.

Still, because she was such a strong woman, Dorothy Hamilton encouraged her son to keep at it, to fight as she was fighting. Scott listened well. As a junior, Scott was anxious to see how much the time

FACT

One of Scott Hamilton's favorite pranks when he was at Rockton's Wagon Wheel was putting shaving cream or whipped cream in the other skaters' skates.

he had lost on the ice because of his injury would hold him back.

Said Scott, "There was some doubt. You never know what effect all that time without being on skates will do, and there was still some pain in the ankle."[4]

Scott was third at the 1975 Midwestern Sectionals. This standing earned him a spot at the nationals in Oakland, California. As Gordie won his third straight title, Scott placed seventh in junior men. Brunet was pleased, because his student's skating was strong, even with a healing ankle.

But Brunet was getting older, and he had a surprise in store for Scott. After the 1975 season ended, he retired from coaching. For a short while, Scott worried he would backslide as a competitive skater without Brunet. But he was lucky. Mary Ludington and Evy Scotvold, who were also teaching at Rockton, became his coaches. They were eager to help Scott continue his improvement, but they also knew the Hamiltons were having problems with the cost of skating.

Scott knew nothing of his parents' money problems as he won regionals and sectionals. He headed to the national championships in Colorado Springs thinking he had a good shot at a medal. And he did have a shot at a medal after compulsories and the

FACT

Today, junior skaters are often good enough to compete against seniors. The 1998 world junior champion, Evgeni Plushenko of Russia, was also third at the world seniors.

technical program. Scott was flying high, on and off the ice.

But then he found out that this might be his last event. The Hamiltons no longer could afford to pay for his skating. Scott was crushed. He did not even feel like finishing nationals. What he did not know was that his mother had stopped in Chicago on her way to Colorado. She met with a wealthy couple who knew of Scott. The couple was also part owner of a rink in Denver where world-famous coach Carlo Fassi worked. They told Scott's mother that they would pay Scott's expenses if he would go train in Denver with Fassi. The couple also asked Scott's mother never to identify them as Scott's benefactors.

On the day of the United States Championships free skate, Scott's mom told him he would not have to quit skating. His championship dreams—his Olympic dreams—would remain alive.

Scott went to the rink without a care in the world. He came off the ice as the United States Junior Figure Skating Champion. This was the beginning of a big year for Scott Hamilton and for Carlo Fassi. Olympic champions Dorothy Hamill and John Curry were both coached by Fassi. Scott Hamilton traveled overseas for the first time to compete. He finished second in a German event and third in a

FACT

Mary Ludington and Evy Scotvold would eventually marry. They have coached many successful skaters, including Nancy Kerrigan and Paul Wylie.

competition in France. For the first time, his coach mentioned the Olympics.

Scott Hamilton graduated from Bowling Green High School in 1976 (two years ahead of his class-mates). He had done enough work through tutoring and special home-study courses to earn his diploma early.

He bought a car and moved into a room where Dorothy Hamill once lived in Denver. The sun was shining everywhere for Scott. Then the dark clouds returned.

His 1977 season, the first as a senior, did not go well. Various injuries slowed him down. He barely made it to nationals by finishing third at midwest-erns. He came in ninth in Hartford, Connecticut. However, few first-year seniors ever did better than that at the United States Championships.

Those nationals were the last competition in which Scott's mom ever saw her son skate. A few weeks later, she and Scott's dad drove to Fort Wayne, Indiana, to see Scott in an exhibition. Scott's mom was very weak from cancer. She was too ill to attend the ice show in Bowling Green that Scott starred in every year. On May 19, 1977, with Scott and his brother, Stephen, in her hospital room, Dorothy Hamilton died.

It was at that point Scott Hamilton promised he

would work his hardest to become the best skater in the world. All the medals he would win would be dedicated to his mother.

"My mom used to tell people how her son would be an Olympic champion," he said. "I owed it to her and to myself and to everyone who supported me to do the best I could."[5]

His best in 1978 was sensational. Hamilton knew that coaches, judges, skating officials, and other skaters were already thinking about 1980. The Olympics would be in the United States that year. He wanted to be on the United States team in Lake Placid, New York.

Hamilton easily qualified for nationals at Portland, Oregon. He was considered a long shot to win a medal there, though. Skaters had jumped from ninth into the top five in the past, but top three?

He was not thinking it was impossible. Scott Hamilton skated superbly and found himself behind only the two favorites, Charlie Tickner and David Santee.

That meant his first trip to the World Championships, in Ottawa, Canada. That also meant performing on the same ice as some of the biggest international stars: Robin Cousins (of Great Britain), Jan Hoffmann (of East Germany) and Irina

Rodnina (of the Soviet Union—considered the greatest pairs skater ever).

Scott had learned from Gordie McKellen never to feel out of place, even in the midst of such famous people. And he did not. He placed an impressive eleventh in his first worlds. Countryman Charlie Tickner took first place.

Once again, though, a good year would be followed by a troubling one. Hamilton learned that Coach Fassi would also be teaching Scott Cramer. The two Scotts were rivals for the third spot on the world team—and eventually the Olympic team. That hurt. So did an ankle ligament injury that cut into Hamilton's training. It seemed as if his world was crashing down again.

"I loved skating and I wanted to keep going, but I couldn't train the way I did before," he said. "And I didn't think anybody cared."[6]

Of course, he was wrong. Scott Hamilton's story had made him a tremendously popular athlete. His fans definitely cared.

His bronze medal at the previous nationals qualified Hamilton for the 1979 championships in Cincinnati, Ohio. He skated well, but not well enough to hold onto third place. David Santee took third as Scott Cramer finished second behind Charlie Tickner.

FACT

Scott Hamilton's first big international win came in the Flaming Leaves competition in November 1979. Flaming Leaves would eventually become known as Skate America. It is the second most important annual skating competition in the United States.

It was time to break with Coach Fassi, Scott Hamilton believed. The Olympic year was coming up, and he needed to be comfortable with his coach. There was so much work to do. Hamilton had become friends with Don Laws, who worked in Philadelphia. Laws invited Scott to move east if he wanted to change coaches. Laws would work with him to prepare for the challenge of making the Olympic squad.

"Don made me feel comfortable about the switch, and he made it clear we would be working hard every day," Hamilton said. "That's exactly what I needed to hear."[7]

The partnership became one of the most successful in American skating. In fact, Scott Hamilton won his first competition working with Laws. He won a gold medal at the Flaming Leaves event in the Lake Placid arena where the Olympic figure skating would be held a few months later.

And how did he win? By finishing first in the technical program and in the free skate. He beat Charlie Tickner, the three-time United States champion. "That was such a big boost," Laws said. "Scott gained so much confidence from winning there, and it carried him through the rest of the year."[8]

At nationals, Scott was ready for anything. He even thought about winning.

He said:

> I realized it was most important to finish in the top three and get on the Olympic team. But I couldn't help thinking I could win. I had so much faith in my skating and in Don's coaching. I really thought I was as good as anyone on the ice, and that was very important for me to get on the team.[9]

Hamilton's footwork had gotten so good that fans clapped and cheered as much for that as for his jumps.

In Atlanta, Georgia, Scott Hamilton expected to do perfect figures, hit every required move in the technical program, and jump through the roof in the free skate. He just about did as he earned the third spot on the United States Olympic team over Scott Cramer (and former coach Fassi).

But Scott Hamilton wondered whether he could compete equally with the world's top skaters. He considered the chances of leaving Lake Placid with a medal.

Even before he would get the chance to answer those questions, Scott received an honor he called "unbelievable." The rest of the United States Olympic team voted him its biggest reward: Scott got to carry the American flag into the opening ceremonies in the Olympic Games in upstate New York.

Scott Hamilton leads the United States Winter Olympics team into position at opening ceremony in Lake Placid, New York, February 13, 1980. Yugoslavia's team stands between the United States team and the team from Russia.

"I was speechless when I found out, and you know how hard it is to make me speechless," he said with a loud laugh. "That was as big an honor as anything I've had."[10] Scott Hamilton carried the flag high. He had become America's skater, and this was perfect proof of his popularity.

Lake Placid became the place for the "Miracle on Ice," when the United States Olympic hockey team shocked the world by beating the powerful Russians to win the gold medal. American speed skater Eric Heiden also won five gold medals in as many races. It would not be Scott Hamilton's golden time, however. Not yet.

Scott Hamilton finished fifth at Lake Placid. But America would not forget him. He was about to become Mr. Figure Skating.

Chapter 4

Building Toward the Gold

It is common after the Olympics for the top skaters to become professionals (no longer eligible for Olympic competition) or to retire. That is what happened after 1980. Robin Cousins, Jan Hoffmann, and Charlie Tickner moved on.

Scott Hamilton headed the men's skating world now. But first, he was headed west, back to Colorado. No, not back to Carlo Fassi as his coach. Fassi left Denver, and Don Laws was hired to coach there. Scott Hamilton joined Laws. Fassi had coached Cousins to gold at Lake Placid. When Cousins retired, he said his choice as favorite for the 1984 Games was none other than Scott Hamilton.

It would not be an easy road to Sarajevo, Yugoslavia, and the next Olympics. There would be many roadblocks Scott Hamilton would need to get past.

Scott and his coach believed it was time to make his programs more athletic. They wanted the programs to look more like a sport and less like a ballet. Scott began to play a bigger role in choosing music and costumes and in putting together his programs.

In order for his style and his approach to skating to make a difference—in order for Scott Hamilton to become a leader in men's figure skating—he needed to be No. 1. He needed to win a national championship, then a world championship. One? How about four?

The first United States crown came in 1981 at San Diego, California. David Santee, who was fourth in the 1980 Olympics, was still around. He was no match, however, for Scott Hamilton's mature, exciting skating show.

On the morning of the technical program, however, Hamilton's dad suffered a stroke in his hotel room. He was in the hospital when his son won the title. But he was able to watch the win on television.

Scott Hamilton's father was hospitalized for a few weeks. Hamilton stayed with him until he was well enough to go home. "My mind was totally on my dad getting better," he recalled. "But he wanted me to concentrate on skating and get ready for worlds."[1]

By the time Scott Hamilton resumed full-time training, he was not sure he could put everything together for worlds. Luckily, they were being held in Hartford, where he had made his senior debut at nationals in 1977. He would not have to travel overseas. Traveling not only took many hours, but also upset the body's timing. Hamilton would also be close by in case his dad needed him.

His main competition would be David Santee, who was second at nationals, and Igor Bobrin of the Soviet Union. And Hamilton trailed going into the free skate. "He had so much confidence at nationals, but now I think Scott had some doubts at worlds," Coach Laws said. "Maybe he was surprised being third or disappointed being third going into the long program. But he's such a great fighter."[2]

He won the free skate, and the competition, despite one fall. It was not his best performance, but it was good enough for gold. At twenty-two, Scott Hamilton was the United States and world champion. Now, he was the man to beat.

All of the skaters below Hamilton would be working hard to catch up and pass him. He had to work just as hard to stay ahead, and make sure he stayed hungry for more gold medals.

When Hamilton returned to his hometown of Bowling Green, he was a hero, the biggest star of the little community. Signs hanging in town told the world that Bowling Green was "Home of World Champion Scott Hamilton."

He was just as popular almost everywhere else. But he was having some problems with being No. 1.

> I guess I let some of the pressure of being on top get to me. I was not the most pleasant person to be around until I got the chance to go for another championship. I felt, for some reason, I hadn't proven myself.[3]

He would feel that way all week at Indianapolis for the 1982 nationals. Heavy snow hit the Indiana capital, and Scott's mood was also stormy. It got even worse after he fell on a double axel. This was a fairly easy jump that he rarely missed in the technical program. Despite the fall, and because he had done so well in compulsory figures, Scott was first overall. And feeling rotten.

"October of 1977, Skate Canada," Scott said of the last time he missed the double axel. "I think I relaxed a little too much. I was shocked. I couldn't believe I went down."[4]

Scott Hamilton knew he could win his second straight United States title even if he did not win the free skate. But that was the last thing he planned on doing. He was going to win the gold by being first in the final portion of the competition.

Scott Hamilton skated through his freestyle program at the United States Figure Skating Championships in Indianapolis, February 1, 1982. Hamilton won his second straight national title.

As Hamilton took the ice and he was introduced, the crowd's roar made it impossible to hear the words. The fans cheered even louder as he hit his first two triple jumps, making it clear he was in control.

Four minutes later, after he spun like a top to finish off a perfect program, it sounded as if the roof of Market Square Arena was about to be blown off. "That's the best I've skated," a breathless Scott said. "I couldn't be happier. I hit everything as clean as could be hit."[5] Nobody could match that. And the worries about being on top were gone.

Next up were the World Championships at Copenhagen, Denmark. There were new challengers now in Norbert Schramm of West Germany and Brian Pockar and Brian Orser, both from Canada. But after that wonderful showing at Indianapolis, Scott again believed strongly in himself.

He also was boosted by the bronze medal won by United States pairs champs Kitty and Peter Carruthers. They were close friends of Hamilton's who had come through the ranks of skating at the same time.

Scott Hamilton's performance at Copenhagen would not match what he did at nationals. It mattered little, however, as he easily won his second world title. By now, Scott Hamilton had won eight straight competitions, an impressive streak.

He did not skate his best in *all* of those victories, and his reputation helped him in some of them. But he won them, and now the Olympics were coming into view.

"I think we really began to think about Sarajevo when the 1983 season began," Scott said. "The programs, the costumes, and the music all were designed to get ready for the Olympics."[6]

One new costume in particular showed how Scott had taken a leadership role in the sport. No more spangles and frills. No more shiny, flowery outfits. This one looked like a warm-up suit, one piece, blue with a red V neck. It might have seemed plain to the audience, but that made sense to Scott, who was especially comfortable in it.

He did not begin wearing it at the start of the '83 season. At Pittsburgh for nationals, Scott won compulsory figures, the technical program, and the free skate—despite missing two triple jumps. A clean sweep from the judges gave him his third United States Championship and a big boost for worlds at Helsinki, Finland.

In Helsinki, Scott first wore the new outfit. He soared to his third straight world title in it, becoming the first American since 1959 to win three in a row.

That costume would become something of a lucky charm for Scott, even though he had begun

FACT

After Robin Cousins won the 1980 Olympics, Carlo Fassi—who had stopped coaching Scott Hamilton in 1979—did not have another Olympic, world, or men's champion in his career. Hamilton went on to win four worlds, four American titles, and one Olympic championship with Don Laws.

Scott Hamilton became the World Champion in the men's singles at the World Figure Skating Championships held in Helsinki, Finland, on March 10, 1983.

winning on the world stage two years before actually putting it on. Everything was in place for a run at the gold medal. Scott began thinking about the 1984 Olympics as soon as the 1983 schedule ended.

"A few of us went to a competition in Zagreb, Yugoslavia, in November, three months before the Olympics," he said. "Then I went to Sarajevo for the first time. It made sense to see where I'd be skating. I'd been to Lake Placid a few months before the '80 Games."[7]

While in Sarajevo, Scott Hamilton tried to imagine what skating as a favorite for gold in the Olympics would be like. He could not imagine it. Nor could he imagine what kind of a send-off he would get at nationals in Salt Lake City. In compulsory figures, he was first with every judge. He had the same results for the technical program. And in the free skate, where he received four perfect scores of 6.0 for artistry, he again swept the judging panel. Scott Hamilton was ready for the Olympics.

Chapter 5

Olympic Champion

In February 1984, the world's greatest athletes on ice and snow came to Sarajevo, Yugoslavia, in the shadow of Mount Bjelasnica, for the Winter Olympics.

Not long after the games, Sarajevo became the center of a terrible civil war that destroyed most of the area. During the Olympics, however, it was a place of celebration.

Much of the talk before the Sarajevo Olympics was about the United States hockey team. Could it repeat its Miracle on Ice, when the Americans upset the powerful Soviet Union to win the gold medal at the 1980 Games in Lake Placid?

There was great interest in Yugoslav alpine skier Juri Franko. He hoped to become the first Winter Olympics medalist from his country. At the Zetra Ice

Arena where figure skating would be held, the focus was on ice dancers Jayne Torvill and Christopher Dean of England. Could they break the gold medal run of the Soviets?

East German teenager Katarina Witt (who would later join the Stars on Ice tour in 1994) would make her first Olympic appearance in a duel for gold with America's Rosalynn Sumners.

And then there was Scott Hamilton. He was already a three-time world champion, and he came to Sarajevo the favorite to win the first men's gold for the United States since the 1960 Olympics.

Americans had won four straight Olympic championships leading up to and including the '60 Games. Then, nothing.

Said Hamilton,

> I knew about that, but when you are on the ice, you are skating for yourself and to do the best you can. You can't be thinking, "I have to win because no American has won since David Jenkins." You have to think about skating your best and letting whatever happens happen.[1]

Hamilton was very famous by 1984. He was known for his jumping and footwork and for the joy he showed on the ice. His life story was told in magazines and newspapers, on radio and television.

The adopted boy who nearly died, whose health

improved when he discovered skating, inspired fans everywhere. They knew of his mother's death and of Hamilton's dedication to his career in honor of his mother.

People remembered Scott Hamilton carrying the American flag at Lake Placid. They saw his victories at San Diego, Indianapolis, Pittsburgh, and Salt Lake City for his four national crowns. And they remembered the World Championship victories in Hartford, Copenhagen, and Helsinki. Now, they wanted to see Scott Hamilton take home a medal at the Olympics.

Hamilton enjoyed the first week of the games. After practice each day, he would watch other events, including skiing and hockey. He said:

> It was important to me to get the whole Olympic experience. I didn't forget I was there to skate, but I also wanted to do the things that make the Olympics special. I wanted to spend time with the other athletes and watch other sports and just have fun.
>
> The great thing about the Olympics for us is that we get to be with hockey players and skiers and sledders. At the other competitions, like nationals and worlds, we're with skaters. At the Olympics, it's different and you want to enjoy it.[2]

In addition to skating, Hamilton was a spectator at other skating events. He cheered for close friends

FACT

The Zetra Ice Arena where Scott Hamilton won his Olympic gold medal was destroyed during the civil war that tore apart Yugoslavia. The arena was bombed during the war and was completely leveled.

Kitty and Peter Carruthers. They wound up second in the pairs, the best United States finish since 1952.

"Scott still was sort of an idol to me," said Rosalynn Sumners. "I wondered if I could live up to what he did. We kind of hung out together with the whole team, and I had put all of them up on a pedestal, with Scott up there the highest."[3]

Also on hand for the Olympics was Hamilton's dad. The Rotary Club in Bowling Green had raised more than two thousand dollars to send Scott Hamilton's father to Sarajevo. Hamilton's main competition was Canada's Brian Orser, Poland's Jozef Sabovcik, and another young American named Brian Boitano.

The men's skating began with compulsories and Scott Hamilton was nervous. He was a master of the free skate and usually unchallenged in the technical program. But the compulsories, those exact tracings of figure eights, gave him the jitters. Still, he traced well on his first figure. And even better on the second. And even better than that on the third.

Hamilton won all three compulsories. This was something he had never done in an international meet. He was feeling even better about his chances for gold. But the next day's practice did not go well. He had trouble with the entire technical program—the jumps, the footwork, and the spins.

"I was a little off, but I thought it would get better when we had to skate the program," he said. It did, but not all that much. He lost the technical program to Brian Orser.

However, he was second in the technical and first overall. This gave him a big lead over Orser, who finished only seventh in compulsories. Scott Hamilton headed into the free skate so far ahead that only a complete wipeout would take away the gold.

By the time the free skate took place, most of the other Olympic questions had been answered. The American hockey team was a flop. Franko won a silver in the giant slalom. Torvill and Dean swept the scoreboard with perfect marks in their free dance.

Hamilton was bothered by an ear infection that made jumping and spinning even harder than they normally were.

Said Scott Hamilton of Brian Orser:

> I came onto the ice after Brian and I knew he'd done very well. There were flowers still lying on the ice that were thrown out there for him. I even picked up a few to loosen up. I wasn't usually nervous at that point in a competition. Not anymore, at least. I'd been in sixteen competitions, so I thought I was past that. But these were the Olympics and my dream of a gold

medal . . . I really wanted to have a lights-out performance.[4]

Hamilton's performance was less than spectacular. He stumbled on a triple Salchow jump and completed only a double. He did a single flip rather than a triple; his timing was off. Still, the crowd loved him. American flags waved everywhere. Fellow skaters watching in the stands stood on their feet when he was done. They joined in as the fans gave Hamilton a huge ovation.

Looking at coach Don Laws, Scott said two words: "I'm sorry." For what? For winning a gold medal? Brian Orser won the free skate, but Scott Hamilton's lead was too big to overcome. Hamilton, the little guy from Bowling Green with the big heart, had joined Dick Button, Hayes Jenkins, and David Jenkins as American figure skating gold medalists at the Olympics.

"I won the Olympics, but I didn't feel it was an Olympic performance," he said. "I knew I could do more than I did that night."[5]

Only a perfectionist like Scott Hamilton could feel that way. He cried on the podium when "The Star-Spangled Banner" was played and when the medal was hung around his neck. He picked up an American flag and held it high in a victory lap around the rink.

FACT

Canadian Brian Orser, who finished second to Hamilton in Sarajevo, and later in his career joined Hamilton's Stars on Ice Tour, was also second to Brian Boitano at the 1988 Olympics. Another Canadian, Elvis Stojko, won the silver medal at the 1994 and 1998 Olympics.

Scott Hamilton won the gold medal in the free skating competition at the 1984 Winter Olympics in Sarajevo. Jozef Sabovcik (left) of Czechoslovakia was awarded the bronze medal and Brian Orser of Canada won the silver medal.

Ten years later, to the day, Scott sat in the Hamar figure skating rink and looked back at that special time in Sarajevo. The arena was practically empty—nearly everyone was next door in the practice rink as Nancy Kerrigan and Tonya Harding skated in the same workout session.

While relaxing in the broadcast booth where he was working for CBS-TV, covering skating, he recalled the following:

> I loved being at the Olympics, skating there, being with the other athletes. It was a very special thing to win the gold medal. As I look back—can you believe it's ten years?—I understand how great it is to achieve something like that. Even if you feel you didn't do as well as you could, you've still done something so special.
>
> As a competitor, you're involved in what *you* do. As a commentator now, you're involved in what everybody else does. And you start to realize how great it was that you got a chance to go for the gold.[6]

Chapter 6

Turning Pro

Scott Hamilton had one more piece of business to clear up before turning professional. Skating his best and winning another world championship were high on his list of priorities. He reflected:

> I had won the gold medal at Sarajevo. It was my career goal, of course, and it was a great feeling. But I didn't skate well at the Olympics, at least not the way I wanted to skate. I always dreamed of having my greatest performance at the Olympics, hitting everything and having the gold medal hanging around my neck, knowing I could never skate like that again. That's not how I felt.[1]

First, Hamilton took a telephone call of congratulations from President Ronald Reagan. Later on, he would visit the White House with other Olympians.

President Ronald Reagan accepts an Olympic parka from Scott Hamilton, the gold medalist in figure skating in the 1984 Olympics while Nancy Reagan looks on during a White House ceremony.

He was invited to throw out the first ball at a New York Yankees game. A street in Bowling Green was named in his honor.

Scott Hamilton was an American hero. Perhaps only he believed there was more work to do.

The 1984 world championships were in Ottawa, Canada. This was the same place where Scott competed in his first worlds and placed eleventh six years earlier. This time, he came to Canada as a four-time American champion, a three-time world champion, and an Olympic gold medalist, riding a seventeen-event winning streak. Still, his less than perfect skate at Sarajevo was eating away at him.

"There was not much pressure on me after Sarajevo," he said. "But I put pressure on myself to do well, because it [the World Championship competition] probably was my last eligible competition and it also was a chance to show how I wanted to skate in the Olympics."[2]

Which he did. Hamilton won compulsories, as he now was expected to do. He also won the technical program with a very strong showing. By the time the free skate—his last free skate at this level—had begun, Scott Hamilton was assured another world crown.

Brian Orser won the long program again (as he had at the Olympics). Scott Hamilton, however,

Scott Hamilton skates past cheering crowd at Zetra's ice rink after being awarded the gold medal in figure skating at the 1984 Winter Games in Sarajevo.

became the first man since Hayes Jenkins (1953–56) to win four worlds. He skated very well, and he was able to leave with a smile. So what was next? He was not quite sure. But he knew he would keep busy.

After officially announcing his retirement from Olympic skating after the 1984 World Championships, Scott Hamilton was honored with a parade in Denver, where he now lived full-time.

In May, he went back to his roots in Bowling Green to headline the International Stars on Ice show. The show raised money for cancer research and was a memorial to Hamilton's mom.

Scott Hamilton wanted to do something special for the crowd at the rink where it all began for him. After a full day of visiting schools and holding news conferences, he headed for the place that made him most comfortable and most secure—the ice.

He appeared in three shows in Bowling Green that May. At the end of the final one, the crowd stood, clapped, and cheered for its local legend. Scott Hamilton unzipped the top of his costume and pulled out a ribbon. Attached to it hung his Olympic gold medal. It was as if he was sharing his dream, his triumph, his wonderful career with the folks back home.

"Scott is the kind of person who, when you meet him for the first time, he makes you feel like you've known him for your whole life," said Kurt Browning, another four-time world champion who was one of the featured performers in Stars on Ice, the tour Scott organized and still leads. "Then, every time you see him again, he makes you feel like a friend."[3]

In 1984, with so much already accomplished, Scott Hamilton joined Ice Capades, one of the two major tours then in existence. Such shows are hard work. Some weeks, Ice Capades had two performances each day. There were very few days off, and the travel was hard. In a week, the tour might hit five cities.

The routines were fun, and Hamilton rarely was on the ice alone. He might be joined by skaters dressed up as cartoon characters, or other members of the cast.

The 1995 United States Men's Championships were held in Kansas City, Missouri. Brian Boitano won the first of four straight crowns. On that very same night Scott Hamilton was making his show debut in Madison Square Garden in New York.

Hamilton wondered what was going on in Kansas City. But he didn't miss being there. He said:

> My whole seventeen years of skating were so worth it. The first time you're announced as national champion is the greatest feeling in the world. I thought I had a few years of competition left. But after winning a gold medal at the

Olympics, after that's done, what's left? And
I'm twenty-six and I thought it was time to
stand on my own two feet.[4]

Yet, he wondered why there had to be a separation, why there had to be a professional level where skaters were not allowed to skate at nationals, worlds, or the Olympics. Why shouldn't skating be like tennis, where all events except those involving school or purely amateur organizations are open to everyone?

"I'm not saying the whole system is wrong, but I'm not sure what it accomplishes. I can understand it on a college level, but not on our level."[5]

There were competitions available for Hamilton, the biggest of which was the World Professional Championships. He finished second in that in 1985 to another Olympic champ, Robin Cousins. He won it for the first time one year later in 1986. But Scott wanted so much more out of his skating. He wanted to make a difference. He understood that winning gold medals and championships would help him do just that.

He said:

Skating is very much a female sport. I want to
break down some of those barriers. The direction I always took in skating was that I wanted
to be for skating what Kurt Thomas was for

gymnastics. You do not want the focus of what you are doing to be what you are wearing. Everything should be balanced. Loud, obnoxious costumes will take people's minds off what you are doing. I think there are too many sequins today. It's an entertainment sport, but why would a man want to go out looking like a woman?

I wanted to introduce the men to the general audience as a very ballistic kind of performer. Lots of jumps, lots of spins. And the only way I could do that was, I had to win. A lot. I never intended to win as many competitions as I did, but it just kind of happened. My style of skating and my direction of skating just happened to be right at the right time.[6]

In 1986, it was not the right time for Scott Hamilton and Ice Capades. His contract was not renewed. He was told that male figure skaters could not be stars in shows, that they could not carry a tour. Hamilton knew better. And this was a challenge—like all those other challenges—that he could sink his teeth into.

"I sat down with Bob [Kain, his business manager] and we thought about what we could do," he said. "There was no tour where skaters could put together their own routines and also work on improving their skating, take it to another level as an artist and a competitor. That was what we felt we could do."[7]

The Scott Hamilton America Tour was born that year. Rosalynn Sumners joined it, not knowing it would turn into the most successful skating show ever. It was the beginning of the Stars on Ice tour, although it would not take that name until Discover Card became its sponsor in 1987.

The America Tour went to five cities in New England. It was a test of the popularity of a show with group numbers, solo performances, theatrical lighting and staging—even conversation between the performers and the audience.

It was a huge success. When Scott Hamilton joined 1976 Olympic champion Dorothy Hamill and Robin Cousins to headline another short tour, Bob Kain suggested a new name: Stars on Ice.

Before the first full Stars on Ice tour began in 1987, Scott Hamilton was in great demand. He appeared in ice shows at the Kennedy Center in Washington, on Broadway, and at various hotel resorts. Sea World in San Diego, California, asked Hamilton to produce two ice shows. The first one was called "Celebration on Ice" and became one of the most popular attractions at the theme park. The second, "Odyssey on Ice," played to nearly one million people in just three months.

Hamilton was also collecting his share of awards. Of course, this was nothing new—when he

FACT

One of Scott Hamilton's favorite routines has always been "Hair." He begins the program wearing a huge wig. He ends it without the wig and by reversing his vest—turning him from hippie to businessman.

was winning all of those national and world titles, he was named United States Olympic Committee (USOC) Athlete of the Year four straight years.

The Olympic Spirit Award, also presented by the USOC, went to Scott Hamilton in 1987. That was followed by one of the most prestigious honors he ever received: the Jacques Favart Award for contributions to skating. It was presented by the International Skating Union (ISU), which runs figure skating and speed skating competitions throughout the world. The Favart prize had been given to only four others before Scott Hamilton: Eric Heiden, who won five gold medals in as many speed skating events at the 1980 Games; Irina Rodnina, three-time Olympic champion in pairs; and the ice dancing team of stars Jayne Torvill and Christopher Dean, who eventually joined Stars on Ice.

"This sport has grown so much and I'm so proud to have been a part of that growth," a visibly moved Hamilton said.[8]

Later on, Katarina Witt, who also would become a cast member of the Discover Card Tour, won the award. Stars on Ice rocketed to the top of the figure skating world, and many other famous champions wanted to join. Through the years, it has featured more world and national champs and Olympic medal winners than any other show.

Scott Hamilton makes a leap toward winning the gold medal in the free skating finals at the Winter Games in Sarajevo.

Said Rosalynn Sumners:

> I think a lot of that is because we're such a family. A lot of it is because everyone wants to skate with Scott. After the Olympics, he did Ice Capades and I did Disney on Ice. Except at professional competitions, we didn't meet. But after two years of Disney, I hated it and wanted to quit. I am not the type who likes to do fourteen shows a week, and we were doing that. I was very homesick and I wasn't able to train or to skate the way I wanted to. I took the summer off. But when the Scott Hamilton America Tour started, I was one of the first ones Scott called. He knew I needed a jumpstart. I didn't really want to skate, so I said I would think about it. But it was only five cities, so I went to do it. Ever since, it has grown each year to be more and more.[9]

Sumners credits Hamilton with boosting her just when she was ready to give up skating. "Scott had this belief in me to keep going," she said. "He made me want to do it, too."[10]

Rosalynn Sumners remains the only original cast member of Stars on Ice—besides Scott Hamilton, of course—who still is with the tour. While Stars on Ice continued to grow, Scott Hamilton won more honors. He was inducted into the World Figure Skating Hall of Fame in 1990, the same year he went into the USOC Hall of Fame.

Scott Hamilton returned home to Denver, Colorado, where a welcoming ceremony was held and a street was named for him in honor of his Olympic gold medal.

"My amateur career was a fantasy," Hamilton said when he joined the most famous of Olympic athletes in the USOC Hall. His Stars on Ice routines had become fantastic. Fans would leave the arena after a show talking about Hamilton's numbers and his back flips, a move that became almost a trademark for him.

There was his "Battle Hymn of the Republic," which Scott Hamilton dedicated to the memory of the United Skates skating team that died in a 1961 plane crash. There was his "Hair," with Hamilton wearing a huge wig and skating to music from the offbeat Broadway musical.

There was his "Barber of Seville" routine. Hamilton lip-synched and skated to "Figaro." There was his "Walk This Way," routine in which he paraded around the ice as a member of the rock group Aerosmith.

What has been most special has been the way Scott Hamilton kept his identity, even while playing all these characters. "The trick is remaining genuine on the ice," he said. "You let people see you, see who you are, what you are."[11]

What Hamilton had become was the king of the ice.

Chapter 7

Skating Legend

By 1990, figure skating was undergoing major changes, and Scott Hamilton was in the middle of them. He was experiencing these changes both as a competitor and as a spokesman.

The professional tour (shows and competitions) had added important events and also welcomed such great skaters as Brian Boitano, Brian Orser, and Katarina Witt to its ranks. Still, it was not as popular as the competitions and championships that would lead to the Olympics. So, for many fans, Scott Hamilton was most visible in his role of television commentator for CBS.

Scott Hamilton joined CBS in 1987. He thought it was a part-time job. It turned out to be much more. Hamilton worked the 1992, 1994, and 1998

Olympics for CBS, and he has starred in prime-time specials.

Scott Hamilton is a natural for broadcasting. His wit, charm, and knowledge of his sport make him one of the true experts in sports television.

He had the following comments on his commentating duties:

> The most important thing for me is being prepared with as much information as possible without stepping on the entire performance when I give out the information. If I had the opportunity to say all that needed to be said so everyone would know everything that was going on, we would need a twelve-minute long program in which I talk wall to wall. I feel each year I've made some improvements in being a commentator. I hope to entertain and enlighten and educate and outline what is going on, then let the performers take over. The skater is trying to let you in on what they are like as a person. I don't want to get in the way. When they put a routine together, they are trying to show a piece of themselves to everyone in the building. I can help by pointing out exactly what they are doing. That's all.[1]

What the skaters were doing in 1991 was quite different from what Scott Hamilton had done. Rules changes had eliminated compulsories. These changes made the technical program (now called the

Scott Hamilton waves his gold medal to the welcoming crowd in Denver, on his return home from the Winter Olympics in Sarajevo.

short program) worth 33 percent of the total score. The free skate (also known as the long program) was worth 67 percent of the total score.

Women such as Midori Ito of Japan and America's Tonya Harding were doing triple axels— a three-and-a-half revolution jump so hard that no other women have ever done it in competition. Men were regularly trying quadruple jumps (four revolutions), and even doing them in combination.

Hamilton worried that artistry and overall balance were disappearing.

> It seems now more than ever jumps are everything. It's always been judged on jumping, but it hasn't been the end-all, be-all like it is now. The long program is sort of a compulsory free program. It allows every skater to show off his strength. So you get a Kurt Browning throwing in two triple axels in one program or a Chris Bowman doing a triple-triple combination. But I think the sport is trying to be too many things, with changes coming too quickly. I'm not the traditionalist . . . but there have been so many radical changes in the sport and it's hard to figure out. . . . Figure skating has a personality and I hope the changes that are being made will not eliminate the personality of the sport.[2]

Scott Hamilton got the chance to become part of the national and World Championships and Olympics again in 1993, but he passed on the opportunity. In

1993, the International Skating Union said it would allow all professionals to return to the eligible ranks for the 1994 season. That, of course, would include the Olympics at Lillehammer, Norway.

Scott Hamilton would be thirty-four years old—old for an Olympic figure skater. He had not trained for the technical and long programs others such as Kurt Browning, Alexei Urmanov, and Elvis Stojko were doing. He could go to Lillehammer for CBS. He liked everything he was doing and how his career and the Stars on Ice tour had taken off. Hamilton made his decision:

> I don't want to compete in the Olympics again. I have no desire to mess with those memories by trying to do it again. I had my time. The sport has changed in its focus since I was competing and I really don't know how I would fit in with that.[3]

Still, he supported the idea of open skating, even if it was just for that one year. The ISU is considering doing it again for the 2002 season and the Salt Lake City Olympics. "It will be great for the sport. . . . When you look at the best athlete, then everyone should be allowed to compete."[4]

Scott Hamilton passed on the Olympics. But he remained busy with his work with the Make-A-Wish Foundation. It is the main charity involved

FACT

After Nancy Kerrigan was attacked and hit on the leg with a tire iron at a practice for the 1994 National Championships, security was tightened at all skating events—including the Stars on Ice tour.

Sometimes Hamilton and the other Stars on Ice skaters used false names when checking into hotels.

with Stars on Ice. The tour has raised millions of dollars for Make-A-Wish, which grants the wishes of gravely ill children. Scott Hamilton has been a leading spokesman. He also makes dozens of appearances a year at hospitals and makes wishes come true for the kids who want to skate with him.

"Anytime you put together a tour with the cast we have, it's nice to do something for somebody else," said Hamilton.[5]

Scott Hamilton also was one of the organizers of Hope, an organization of Olympic athletes that raised funds for the survivors of war-torn Sarajevo. He said,

> I have so many great memories from Sarajevo. But it's not the same place now. It's tragic what has happened there, and if any of us can help even one person there, we'll have done something worthwhile.[6]

While Hamilton was in Lillehammer, broadcasting the end of the Tonya Harding–Nancy Kerrigan feud, his father grew very ill. Ernie Hamilton had moved to Florida five years earlier, and on the last day of February, he died.

Scott Hamilton rushed from Lillehammer to Florida for the funeral. He was older now than he had been when his mother died. He was an established star, an Olympic champion, and he knew he owed everything to his parents. They had always been his biggest fans.

The night of the funeral, Scott Hamilton flew to Madison Square Garden in New York for the Stars on Ice show. "I had to," he said. "I knew my dad would have wanted me to, expected me to be there. And I skated for him that night, and for my mom."[7]

Later in 1994, Hamilton was given an honorary doctoral degree from Bowling Green State, the university at which both of his parents had taught. He was the keynote speaker to the graduating class. He told the graduates how "you must fight for everything you believe in if you want to succeed."[8]

Scott Hamilton had become a huge success. Figure skating's popularity exploded after the Lillehammer Games, and he was in the middle of it. Every television network wanted to broadcast competitions, and they wanted the most famous skaters in them. Hamilton performed in a bunch of the made-for-television events, and they drew big ratings. America could not get enough of figure skating.

Scott Hamilton has also guided Stars on Ice to the top. By 1995, the tour traveled to as many as sixty cities in a season. He had his own television specials, including "Scott Hamilton . . . Upside Down," in which he acted and skated. He was also doing skating commentary. Life was busy. Life was sweet. Then tragedy struck again. Twice.

In November 1995, while rehearsing for the opening show of the Stars on Ice tour, Sergei Grinkov collapsed in the Lake Placid ice rink and died of a heart attack. A close friend of Hamilton's, Grinkov was only twenty-eight.

Grinkov and his wife, Ekaterina Gordeeva, had joined the tour four years before. The two-time Olympic pairs champions were part of the Stars family. They were part of Scott Hamilton's extended family, too.

"Sergei was a devoted father and husband and friend, and one of the greatest guys I've ever met," said Hamilton. "He could make you laugh and he was a great audience, too. Nothing in my life ever hit me so hard."[9]

The entire 1995–96 tour was dedicated to Grinkov. On February 27, 1996, Gordeeva returned to the ice in "A Celebration of a Life." It was a special performance of the tour in Hartford, Connecticut, during which each skater's routine was a particular favorite of Grinkov's.

Scott Hamilton performed his "Hair" number. But he was most impressed by Gordeeva's loving tribute to her departed husband. She skated to Mahler's Fifth Symphony.

Olympic skaters Kristi Yamaguchi, Katarina Witt, Kurt Browning, and Scott Hamilton appear at New York's Harley-Davidson Cafe to promote "Stars on Ice" at Madison Square Garden.

"I don't think any of us can fathom the amount of strength and courage it took for Katya to come out tonight and perform, and to share her soul with all of us," Hamilton said after the show.[10]

Scott Hamilton would need similar strength and courage for the biggest battle of his life a year later. And as anyone would have expected, Hamilton would win, overcoming cancer to return to the ice.

As the 1997–98 Stars on Ice tour neared the end, Scott Hamilton was thinking about retiring. He still loved the performances and thrilling the crowd, but his body was rebelling. It became tougher to stay in shape, and he worried that the quality of his skating had diminished.

The tour came to Madison Square Garden on March 14, 1998. Hamilton had skated there more than fifty times, but this would be a special night. He just did not know it.

Secretly, Garden officials planned to induct Scott Hamilton into the Wall of Fame. It is Madison Square Garden's way of honoring the best athletes and performers who appeared at the arena. Madison Square Garden officials choose the honorees, and their names are posted on a Wall of Fame near the main entrance to the building. No figure skater had been so honored, but Hamilton would join such great athletes and entertainers as Muhammad

FACT

Scott Hamilton's partner on CBS television's skating broadcasts is Verne Lundquist, who also has done basketball, football, and golf commentary for the network.

Ali, Michael Jordan, Wayne Gretzky, Elton John, and Billy Joel.

The show concluded before a sold-out arena, and the cast members were taking their final bows. Kristi Yamaguchi was handed a microphone. While Scott Hamilton stood with the other skaters, Yamaguchi spoke of a special announcement. Then she introduced Madison Square Garden vice-president Bobby Goldwater.

After a short speech, Goldwater called on Scott Hamilton and handed him a plaque as the newest member of the Wall of Fame. For one of the few times in his life, Hamilton was almost speechless—almost.

> I am totally at a loss. Being here and performing here—and there is no better audience in the world than a New York audience—you've given me goose bumps.
>
> This sheet of ice has had so many incredible moments for me and this is another—to see a show I started twelve years ago be filled to the rafters tonight is *the best.*
>
> It's been kind of a real rough year for me and it's been good to do the entire tour. But the show that means the most is this show.[11]

He paused, perhaps thinking back through all the years, from Bowling Green to Lake Placid, from Sarajevo to Stars on Ice. Could he leave all those memories now? Could he really retire from skating?

Scott Hamilton reacts to the surprise announcement that he was inducted into the Wall of Fame at Madison Square Garden on March 14, 1998. Skaters (left to right) Jayne Torvill, Kurt Browning, Ekaterina Gordeeva, Rosalynn Sumners and Elena Bechke congratulate Hamilton after the Discover Stars on Ice show.

"You've just turned it all around," he told the crowd. "And I'm going to tour next year, for sure."[12]

The Garden crowd erupted in cheers. Scott Hamilton hugged Kristi Yamaguchi and the rest of his skating family on the ice. And as he took a few laps around the rink, holding up the plaque, it was hard to imagine that he would ever hang up his skates.

Chapter Notes

Chapter 1. Hamilton's Greatest Triumph

1. Beth Harris, "Scott Hamilton Returns to the Ice," The Associated Press, electronic news release, October 29, 1997.

2. Author interview with Scott Hamilton, September 16, 1997.

3. Ibid.

4. Ibid.

5. Author interview with Rosalynn Sumners, February 18, 1998.

6. Scott Hamilton, "Fighting Heart," *People*, September 8, 1997, pp. 73–78.

7. Author interview with Kristi Yamaguchi, March 8, 1998.

8. Author interview with Scott Hamilton, September 16, 1997.

9. Ibid.

10. Ibid.

11. Ibid.

12. Ibid.

13. Ibid.

14. Ibid.

15. Author interview with Brian Boitano, March 8, 1998.

16. Author interview with Scott Hamilton, September 16, 1997.

17. Harris, Associated Press electronic news release.

18. Ibid.

19. Ibid.

Chapter 2. Childhood Years

1. Author interview with Scott Hamilton, May 3, 1995.

2. Michael Steere, *Scott Hamilton* (New York: St. Martin's Press, 1985), p. 10.

3. Linda Shaughnessy, *Fireworks on Ice* (Parsippany, N.J.: Crestwood House, 1997), p. 12.

4. Steere, p. 20.

5. Ibid.

6. Author interview with Scott Hamilton, May 3, 1995.

7. Ibid.

8. Author interview with Scott Hamilton, May 3, 1995.

Chapter 3. The First Olympics

1. Author interview with Scott Hamilton, May 3, 1995.

2. Michael Steere, *Scott Hamilton* (New York: St. Martin's Press, 1985), p. 40.

3. Author interview with Scott Hamilton, February 16, 1994.

4. Author interview with Scott Hamilton, May 3, 1995.

5. Author interview with Scott Hamilton, February 16, 1994.

6. Steere, p. 50.

7. Author interview with Scott Hamilton, February 16, 1994.

8. "Hamilton's Long Climb," The Associated Press, electronic news release, February 3, 1984.

9. Ibid.

10. Author interview with Scott Hamilton, May 3, 1995.

Chapter 4. Building Toward the Gold

1. "Hamilton's Long Climb," The Associated Press, electronic news release, February 3, 1984.

2. Ibid.

3. Author interview with Scott Hamilton, May 3, 1995.

4. Michael Steere, *Scott Hamilton* (New York: St. Martin's Press, 1985), p. 249.

5. Ibid.

6. Author interview with Scott Hamilton, May 3, 1995.

7. Ibid.

Chapter 5. Olympic Champion

1. Author interview with Scott Hamilton, February 16, 1994.

2. Ibid.

3. Author interview with Rosalynn Sumners, February 18, 1998.

4. Author interview with Scott Hamilton, February 16, 1994.

5. Ibid.

6. Ibid.

Chapter 6. Turning Pro

1. Author interview with Scott Hamilton, February 16, 1994.

2. Ibid.

3. Author interview with Kurt Browning, October 2, 1997.

4. Terry Taylor, "U.S. Skates-Professionals," The Associated Press, electronic news release, January 30, 1985.

5. Author interview with Scott Hamilton, February 16, 1994.

6. Ibid.

7. Author interview with Scott Hamilton, May 3, 1995.

8. "Hamilton Honored by ISU," The Associated Press, electronic news release, March 26, 1988.

9. Author interview with Rosalynn Sumners, February 18, 1998.

10. Ibid.

11. Author interview with Scott Hamilton, May 3, 1995.

Chapter 7. Skating Legend

1. Author interview with Scott Hamilton, March 8, 1990.

2. "Scott Hamilton on Reinstatement," The Associated Press, electronic news release, May 14, 1993.

3. Ibid.

4. Ibid.

5. Author interview with Scott Hamilton, February 16, 1994.

6. Ibid.

7. Author interview with Scott Hamilton, May 3, 1995.

8. Ibid.

9. Author interview with Scott Hamilton, September 16, 1997.

10. Ibid.

11. Scott Hamilton's speech, Madison Square Garden, March 14, 1998.

12. Ibid.

Career Highlights

Olympic-Eligible Competitions		
YEAR	EVENT	PLACE
1977	U.S. Championships	9th
1978	U.S. Championships World Championships	3rd 11th
1979	U.S. Championships	4th
1980	U.S. Championships Olympics World Championships	3rd 5th 5th
1981	U.S. Championships World Championships	1st 1st
1982	U.S. Championships World Championships	1st 1st
1983	U.S. Championships World Championships	1st 1st
1984	U.S. Championships Olympics World Championships	1st 1st 1st

Professional Competitions

YEAR	EVENT	PLACE
1986	World Professional Championships	1st
1990	U.S. Open	1st
1991	World Professional Championships U.S. Open	2nd 2nd
1993	Hershey's Kisses Pro-Am	2nd
1994	Fox Rock 'n' Roll Championships The Gold Championships	1st 1st
1995	Legends of Figure Skating The Gold Championships Fox Rock 'n' Roll Championships	1st 3rd 1st
1996	Legends of Figure Skating The Gold Championships	1st 2nd

Tours and Ice Shows

YEAR	EVENT
1968	Ice Horizons, Bowling Green, Ohio
1984–86	Ice Capades
1986	Scott Hamilton America Tour
1987–	Discover Card Stars on Ice

Where to Write Scott Hamilton

Mr. Scott Hamilton
c/o Michael Sterling & Associates
4242 Van Nuys Blvd.
Sherman Oaks, CA 91403-3710

On the Internet at:

\<http://www.acor.org/TCRC/scotth.html\>

\<http://proskate.tqn.com\>

Glossary

cancer—A disease that attacks the blood cells and organs of the body and can be fatal.

chemotherapy—A treatment to fight cancer that involves the use of chemicals.

compulsory figures—The tracing of figure eights on the ice. These figures are no longer done in overall competition.

cystic fibrosis—A disease involving defects of various body tissues, including the sweat glands and mucous glands, which makes it difficult to breathe.

double axel—A difficult jump in competition that requires an extra half turn in the air. It is a two-and-a-half revolution jump. The axel is the only jump that begins from the forward outside edge of the skate. It is landed on the back outside edge of the opposite foot.

figure eight—A skating pattern in which a performer's motions form the shape of the number eight on the ice.

free skate—The second portion of competition for solo and pairs skaters. It is worth two thirds of the skater's total score, and skaters may perform anything they choose—within the rules of figure skating.

intermediate level—The easiest level of skating for a serious figure skater. This level is followed by the novice level.

International Skating Union (ISU)—The governing body for international figure skating and speed skating.

junior level—The level of skating for serious figure skaters that follows novice level.

long program—*See also*, free skate.

National Championships—The event in which the top novice, junior, and senior level skaters compete for United States titles.

novice level—The level of skating for serious figure skaters that follows intermediate level.

pairs—A team of skaters composed of one male and one female. The team performs together in competitions. Pairs skating differs from ice dancing in that in pairs, skaters are permitted to do lifts above the shoulder, throws, and jumps.

quadruple jump—Any jump requiring four turns in the air.

regionals—The first level of competition on the way to nationals.

sectionals—The level that follows regionals. Medal winners in sectionals automatically go to the national championships.

senior level—The highest level of skating for serious figure skaters.

stroke—A sudden attack of disease or illness, often involving the brain or nerves.

technical program—The first of two programs skated by solo and pairs skaters. It is worth one third of the total score. There are eight required moves in a technical program.

triple Salchow—A jump in which the skater takes off from the back inside edge of one foot and lands backward on the outside edge of the opposite foot. The skater performs three turns in the air.

tumor—A growth in the body caused by overproduction of cells in a specific area.

United States Championships—The highest prize in Olympic-eligible competitions in American figure skating.

United States Olympic Committee (USOC)—The governing body for Olympic sports in the United States.

World Championships—An important yearly event in figure skating where top Olympic-level skaters from around the world compete.

World Professional Championships—An important yearly competition for professional skaters who are no longer eligible for the Olympics.

Index